Gandhi
The Peaceful Revolutionary

Anna Claybourne

HODDER
Wayland

an imprint of Hodder Children's Books

© 2002 White-Thomson Publishing Ltd

Produced by White-Thomson Publishing Ltd
2/3 St Andrew's Place, Lewes, BN7 1UP

Editor: Anna Lee
Cover Design: Tim Mayer
Inside Design: Tim Mayer
Picture Research: Shelley Noronha –
   Glass Onion Pictures
Proofreader: Philippa Smith

Cover: Gandhi photographed in 1941
Title page: Gandhi in South Africa in 1914

Published in Great Britain in 2002 by Hodder Wayland,
an imprint of Hodder Children's Books

Titles in this series:
Fidel Castro: Leader of Cuba's Revolution
Diana: The People's Princess
Anne Frank: Voice of Hope
Nelson Mandela: Father of Freedom
Mother Teresa: Saint of the Slums
Muhammad Ali: The Greatest
Pope John Paul II: Pope for the People
The Queen Mother: Grandmother of a Nation
John Lennon: Voice of a Generation

British Library Cataloguing in Publication Data
   Claybourne, Anna
   Mahatma Gandhi. - (Famous lives)
   1. Gandhi, M. K. (Mohandas Karamchand), 1869-1948
   2. Statesmen - India - Biography - Juvenile literature
   3. India - Politics and government - 1919-1947 -
   Juvenile literature I. Title
   954'.035'092
   ISBN 0 7502 3954 9

Printed and bound in Italy by G. Canale & C.S.p.A.

Hodder Children's Books
An imprint of Hodder Headline Limited
338 Euston Road, London, NW1 3BH

Picture acknowledgements
The publisher would like to thank the following for their
kind permission to use these pictures: AKG 11; Associated
Press 32; British Library, London/Bridgeman Art Library 8;
Camera Press 27 (bottom); Corbis (cover), 19, 25, 33;
Hodder Wayland Picture Library 15, 21, 36; Hulton
Deutsch 28 (bottom), 29; Hulton Getty 12, 17, 30;
Illustrated London News Picture Library 39; Images of
India 23, 45; Paul Popper 40, 44; Popperfoto 7, 14, 22,
24, 26, 27 (top), 28 (top), 31, 35 (bottom), 37, 42, 43;
Topham Picturepoint (title page) 4, 5, 6, 9, 10, 13, 16, 18,
20, 34, 35 (top), 41. The map on page 38 is by Tim Mayer.

This book is to be returned on or before
the last date stamped below.

CLAYBOURNE
Gandhi - The
Peaceful
Revolution

CLAYBOURNE
Gandhi - The Peaceful Revolution

Contents

A Handful of Salt

It is 6 April 1930, and the sun is beating down on the beach at Dandi, on India's west coast. A small, thin, 60-year-old man, wearing a white robe, wire-rimmed spectacles and simple sandals, walks towards the sea, leading thousands of followers. As they reach the water's edge, the man crouches and picks up a handful of salt, left there by the evaporating sea water.

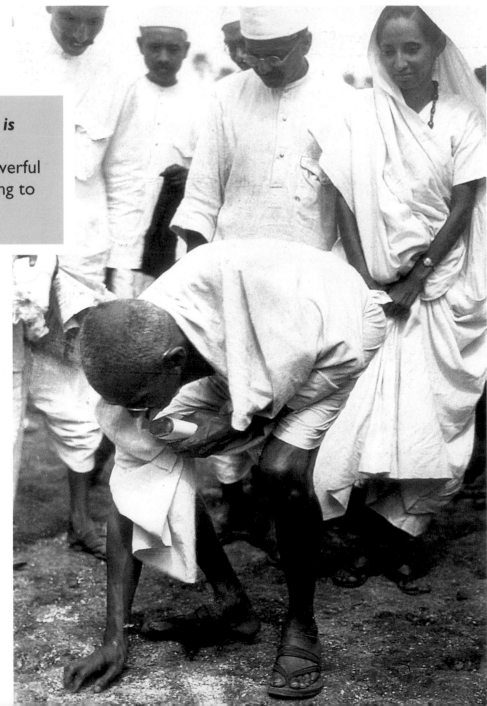

'Mass civil disobedience is like an earthquake.'
Gandhi describing the powerful effects of a people choosing to disobey their rulers.

Gandhi gathers the first handful of salt on the beach at Dandi. He was breaking the law forbidding Indians to collect their own salt.

Picking up salt from a beach may seem an unremarkable act. Yet that day on the beach at Dandi was a turning-point in India's history. The man picking up salt was Mohandas K. Gandhi, known as Mahatma, or 'Great Soul'. By collecting salt, he was defying the British leaders who ruled India at the time. They had passed a law that Indians could not collect their own salt, but had to buy it at a high price.

Gandhi called on all Indians to disobey British laws until India was granted independence. Instead of violent riots, he believed in civil disobedience — a calm, peaceful refusal to co-operate with the government. His ideas were to change India, and the world, for ever.

A photograph of Mahatma Gandhi in 1931, wearing his simple white robe.

Born in the British Empire

Mohandas Gandhi was born in Porbandar, on the north-west coast of India, in 1869. He was the youngest of four children. Gandhi's father was the prime minister of Porbandar state, a tiny traditional kingdom, and his family was reasonably well-off. However, they belonged to the *Vaishya* caste, which is one of the lower social groups in traditional Indian society.

'To believe in something, and not to live it, is dishonest.'
Gandhi explaining how his beliefs affected the way he lived his life.

Mohandas Gandhi aged about seven. He showed his gentle, yet stubborn nature early in life.

In 1869, India was part of the British Empire. That meant it had been taken over by the British. They made the laws, ran the government, and took India's natural riches for themselves. There were many little kingdoms like Porbandar, but they too were under British control.

While he was growing up, Gandhi was deeply affected by his mother's Hindu religion and by the traditions of Porbandar. Hindus, who believe in many gods, are mostly vegetarian, and some Hindus also believe it is wrong to harm any living thing. As a child, Gandhi climbed mango trees in the garden to put bandages on bruised fruits.

This photograph from the days of the British Empire shows two British men having tea in India, attended by three Indian servants.

7

An Early Marriage

In 1882, when he was only thirteen, Gandhi was married. It was a traditional Hindu wedding, to a girl chosen by his family. Her name was Kasturbai Makanji and she was the daughter of a Porbandar cloth-seller.

Later in his life, Gandhi said that his marrying so young had not been a very good idea. He was too young, and still had a lot of growing up to do. He wasn't sure how to be a good husband, and, like any teenager, enjoyed spending a lot of time with his friends. Although he was a bright student, he did very poorly at school during the first year of his marriage.

This painting from around 1887 shows a traditional Hindu wedding.

When he was sixteen, two events changed Gandhi's life. His beloved father, Karamchand Gandhi, died after a long illness, and Gandhi never forgave himself for not being at his father's bedside. Soon afterwards, Kasturbai gave birth to their first child. Sadly, the baby died only a few days later. Gandhi realized it was time to grow up and start taking his education seriously.

Gandhi aged about fourteen, with a friend. Gandhi is on the left.

An English Education

In 1888, when Gandhi was eighteen, he went to London, England, to study law. Friends and family donated money for the trip, so that young Mohandas could have a good education and possibly follow in his father's footsteps as the next prime minister of Porbandar. Gandhi left behind his wife, his new baby son Harilal, and his anxious mother. She was worried that her son would eat meat and drink alcohol, which are both forbidden to Hindus. Gandhi promised her he would remain true to his religion.

At first Gandhi was very shy, but he soon began to enjoy British life. He spent money on expensive Western suits and bow ties, had his hair cut in an English style and learned English manners.

Gandhi (bottom right), dressed in smart Western clothes, with members of the Vegetarian Society in London. Gandhi made some good friends among members of the society.

'The Gita *is not only my Bible or my Koran, it is more than that, it is my mother.'*
Gandhi describing the *Bhagavadgita*, which he called the *Gita*.

However, after about two years, he returned to his Indian roots. He read the *Bhagavadgita*, an ancient Hindu text that urges the faithful to give up material things. He began to live as cheaply as possible, eating the simplest food and walking instead of taking buses. In 1891 Gandhi returned to India, a fully qualified lawyer.

An illustration from a Hindu holy book, the Bhagavata-Purana. *While in London, Gandhi studied the ancient Hindu texts of his homeland.*

An African Adventure

Back in India, Gandhi had trouble finding a job. He moved to Bombay to look for work, with little luck. Life became even more difficult when he tried to become involved in a court case concerning his brother, Laxmidas, and offended a British official. When a law firm in South Africa wrote to offer him a job for a year, he had no choice but to accept.

Gandhi sailed to South Africa in April, 1893. When he arrived he took a train to Pretoria to start his new job. During the journey, a white man objected to his presence in a first-class carriage, and had him thrown off the train. Left to shiver on an empty station all night, Gandhi resolved to fight for the rights of Indians in South Africa.

A steam train emerges from a tunnel in South Africa in the year 1889. The British brought steam railways to many parts of the British Empire. Indians often worked on the railroads in South Africa.

While continuing his legal work, Gandhi began campaigning for better conditions for South Africa's many Indian workers. He soon fetched his family from India, and was to stay in Africa for more than twenty years.

In 1899, the Boer War broke out between British and Dutch settlers in South Africa. Like many Indians, Gandhi joined the war effort on the British side.

'I discovered that as a man and as an Indian I had no rights.'
Gandhi on his first encounter with racial discrimination in South Africa.

Gandhi (middle row, centre) in the Indian Ambulance Corps during the Boer War (1899-1902).

Campaigning for Indians

In the 1890s, South Africa, like India, was a part of the British Empire, and many Indians went to work there. However, they were often treated with disrespect. As well as being banned from travelling first-class, they were insulted with racist nicknames, had an evening curfew and could not vote. They were also forced to pay three pounds — six months' salary — to come and work in South Africa.

Gandhi took up the Indian cause with tireless energy. He wrote letters to newspapers, organized protests and petitions, and founded a campaign group, the Natal Indian Congress, to fight for Indians' rights.

Gandhi was determined to improve the lives of Indian workers in South Africa, such as those pictured below.

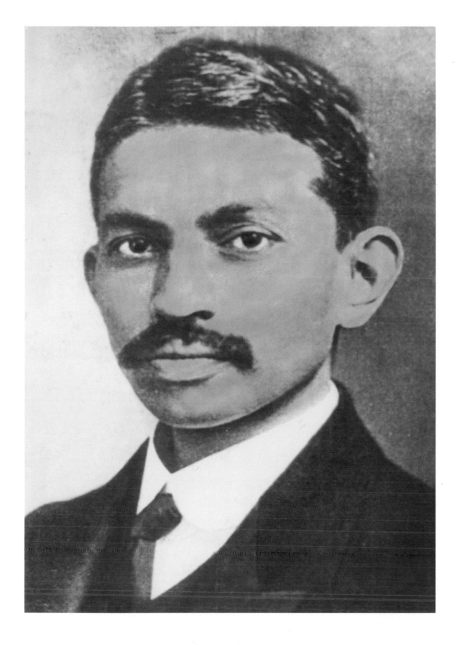

Gandhi as a young lawyer and campaigner in South Africa, when he still wore smart Western clothes.

'Thus the lynching ultimately proved to be a blessing for me.' Gandhi on being beaten up by an anti-Indian mob. He forgave his attackers and called for them to be spared from punishment, which increased public sympathy for him.

Gandhi's career in his law offices in Pretoria was going well, but he was also well-known for his political activities. Returning from a trip to India in 1897, he was met by an angry crowd at the docks. They beat him and pelted him with bricks and rotten fish, claiming he intended to flood South Africa with Indians.

Gandhi was almost beaten to death, but was saved by the police. After the incident, the press supported his campaign, and he grew more popular than ever amongst the Indians in South Africa.

The Simple Life

Over the years, Gandhi improved life for Indians in South Africa. At the same time, he began to make changes in his own life, gradually changing himself into the simply-dressed, monk-like figure he is remembered as today.

He began by cutting his own hair and cleaning his own bathroom. According to Hindu tradition, these tasks should only be performed by Untouchables – the lowest members of society.

Gandhi in South Africa in 1914, wearing a cotton tunic – the first version of his famous plain white outfit.

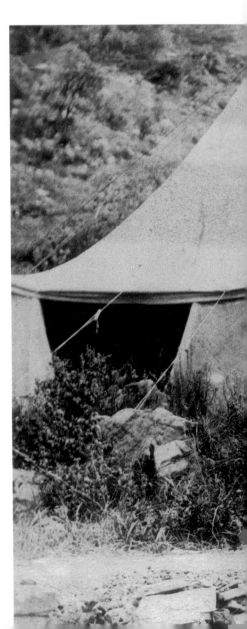

Gandhi (bottom right) set up this ashram, a kind of communal farm, near the city of Johannesburg. There he and his followers ate simply, prayed, studied and shared everyday tasks.

At first, Gandhi's wife Kasturbai did not approve, but he asked her to do the same. He fed his family on a basic diet of fruit and nuts, and he often fasted completely. He also began to wear plain, white clothes.

After reading the works of philosophers such as John Ruskin and Henry Thoreau, Gandhi developed the idea of winning political battles through non-violent civil disobedience. He used the term *Satyagraha*, meaning 'truth-force', to describe this approach, and encouraged Indians in South Africa to use it in their campaigns.

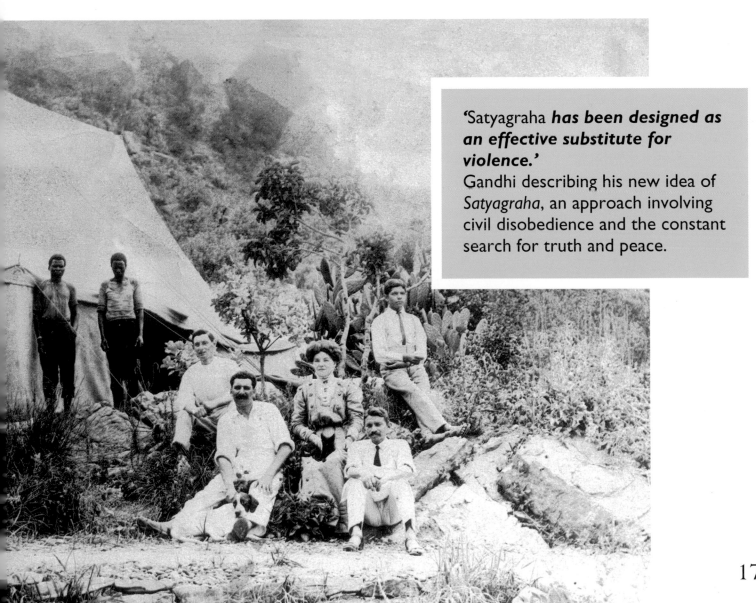

'Satyagraha *has been designed as an effective substitute for violence.'*
Gandhi describing his new idea of *Satyagraha*, an approach involving civil disobedience and the constant search for truth and peace.

Back to India

In 1914, Gandhi negotiated new conditions for Indians with General Smuts, the South African Prime Minister. Indian marriages, which had been made unlawful, were made legal again, and the charge for working in South Africa was abolished. Gandhi and Kasturbai decided it was time to go home to India. Gandhi was forty-four – more than halfway through his life.

Having proved himself as a campaigner in South Africa, Gandhi now had a new cause. He wanted independence for India.

Gandhi and his wife Kasturbai in Bombay (now called Mumbai) in 1915, soon after they arrived back in India. Kasturbai now agreed with her husband's ideas and was loyal to his simple lifestyle.

'... **not only is** Swaraj **our birthright, but it is our sacred duty to win it.'**
Gandhi talking about the need for *Swaraj* – or independence – in India.

Gandhi addressing an outdoor meeting of his countrymen in Calcutta in May, 1919. At this early stage in his career, Gandhi still occasionally wore British-style clothing.

Soon after his return in 1915, he began to travel the country, protesting against British rule and calling for *Swaraj* (independence). He fought for better conditions for poor weavers, and went on a fast until he won them a wage increase. He also set up a new communal farm, or ashram, near Ahmadabad. Gandhi and some of his followers lived here together, following Gandhi's example of a simple lifestyle and sharing work equally.

Traditional Hindu society has a caste system, which places people at different levels, or *jati*. At the bottom of the pile are the Untouchables, who have to do all the worst jobs and are considered too unclean to touch. Gandhi had always questioned this idea, even as a child. Despite the protests of some of his followers, Gandhi welcomed Untouchables into the ashram to show that he believed all people were equal.

The Great Soul

While travelling around India, Gandhi visited a school run by the great Indian poet Rabindranath Tagore. It was Tagore who gave Gandhi the nickname Mahatma, which means 'Great Soul' in the ancient Indian language, Sanskrit. From then on he was known as Mahatma Gandhi, as he is still known today.

'I have never, even in my dream, thought that I was Mahatma and that others were Alpatma **[little souls]**.' Gandhi modestly denying that the title 'Mahatma' had made him conceited.

Gandhi in his later life with his friend, the poet Rabindranath Tagore. Tagore taught students at his school to dance and weave flower garlands. Gandhi thought they should be doing more useful tasks, such as cleaning the toilets.

During the First World War (1914-18), Indian soldiers fought in the British army in Europe. After the war, many Indians felt India deserved to be granted independence in return for its help.

Gandhi knew that *Satyagraha* and civil disobedience could help to win independence. He urged ordinary Indians to become *Satyagrahi*, or followers of the truth, and called on them to resist British rule by going on strike. News of his hunger strikes and protest speeches spread across the country by word of mouth, radio and newspaper reports. Huge crowds gathered in peaceful protest at some of India's holiest sites.

In 1919 British troops fired on a crowd of peaceful protesters in Amritsar, killing over 300 people. Gandhi was horrified. He called off the strikes, determined to win independence without bloodshed.

This picture shows Indian soldiers in the British army in France, during the First World War of 1914-18.

The Cloth Campaign

By 1920, Gandhi was famous. He spoke to huge crowds numbering hundreds of thousands, encouraging them not to pay British taxes or wear British clothes. This was the beginning of a new campaign called the cloth campaign. The Mahatma urged the public to burn their old British-style clothes, and instead spin their own thread on a traditional Indian spinning wheel, or *charkha*.

'The truest test of civilization, culture, and dignity is character, not clothing.'
Gandhi pointing out, as part of his cloth campaign, that modern Western clothes did not make their wearers better than anyone else.

Gandhi spinning his own khadi (cloth) on a charkha (spinning wheel). He now described himself as a 'farmer and weaver', not a lawyer.

Gandhi during a fast in 1924, which he began as a protest against the violence between Hindus and Muslims. The girl in the picture is Indira Gandhi, who later became India's prime minister. She was not Gandhi's daughter, but the daughter of his friend Jawaharlal Nehru.

By the end of 1919, Gandhi had joined forces with the official independence movement, the Indian National Congress. The group adopted the *charkha* as its symbol. When violence broke out again in 1922, Gandhi was arrested and imprisoned.

When he was released two years later, the movement had died down. Gandhi revived it with more demonstrations and speaking tours, and went on another hunger strike to stop fighting between Hindus and Muslims. Unlike Hindus, who believe in many gods, Muslims believe there is only one god, whose name is Allah. Since Hindus and Muslims shared many of the same areas of India, there was often tension between them. In 1925, Gandhi was elected president of the Indian National Congress.

India Unites

A protest march through the streets of Bombay (now Mumbai) in 1930. The women in the procession are wearing white homespun clothes and carrying signs urging people to boycott British goods.

Gandhi was now almost sixty years old, and had a new nickname, *Bapu*, which means 'grandpa'. Everyone in India knew who he was, and millions were joining in with his civil disobedience campaign. They refused to buy British goods or pay taxes, went on strike from their jobs and attended huge rallies to hear Gandhi speak.

> **'Non-co-operation with evil is as much a duty as co-operation with good.'** Gandhi justifying the principle of non-co-operation and civil disobedience.

Gandhi in front of a crowd of protestors. Sometimes he made a speech, but sometimes he simply stood in silence with his hands together, inspiring the crowd with this simple demonstration of peaceful protest.

However, 'Bapu' was suffering from exhaustion. He had given up the presidency of the Indian National Congress at the end of 1925, and was often unwell. He was also upset when anti-British riots broke out, as they often did. He still wanted a completely non-violent victory.

Finally, the viceroy (British controller) of India, Baron Irwin, agreed to meet with Gandhi. But Irwin's hands were tied, since the British government would not grant him the power to give in to Indian demands. In the end, Gandhi and the Indian National Congress decided to declare independence themselves, on 31 December 1929.

The Salt Struggle

Although the Congress had declared
independence the British government did not
agree, and the boycotts and riots continued. So
Gandhi began planning a new *Satyagraha*, which
was to become his most famous struggle.

On 12 March 1930, Gandhi and a
group of followers set off from his
ashram, the communal farm where
he lived, near Ahmadabad. They
were heading for the coast. As they
walked, Gandhi preached his
beliefs, urging people to spin their
own cloth, avoid meat and alcohol,
and disobey the British. They
gathered supporters on the way,
and when they reached Dandi there
were thousands of marchers.

When Gandhi bent and picked up
the first handful of salt from Dandi
beach, he sent a message around
the world that Indians would no
longer bow to British laws.

*Gandhi on the famous salt
march, accompanied by
supporters and friends.*

In this picture, Gandhi's followers are making salt from seawater by putting it in dishes to evaporate in the sun.

Across the country, people began collecting their own salt, instead of buying heavily taxed salt from the British as they were supposed to by law. There were more riots, protests and arrests, but the salt march worked. Gandhi was imprisoned for starting the campaign, but after his release the following year, he was invited to Britain to take part in independence talks.

A riot in the streets of Calcutta, in eastern India, sparked by Gandhi's release from prison in early 1931.

Gandhi in Britain

Gandhi went to Britain in 1931 to take part in a conference on Indian independence. Many British people were in favour of granting India its freedom, and the government had decided to address the question.

However, the trip was really more useful for Gandhi as a publicity exercise. The British press and public loved him, and his visit was reported around the world. He made a speech in Oxford, visited factory workers, met the film star Charlie Chaplin, and had tea with King George V – all dressed in his usual white robes.

This picture shows Gandhi with the film star Charlie Chaplin, at the house of an Indian friend in London.

Gandhi emerging from a taxi in London in 1931, to be greeted by a crowd of supporters and journalists.

Gandhi with British workers on a visit to Lancashire in England.

The conference itself was not such a success. It was impossible to work out how to divide up power between different groups – especially Hindus and Muslims – in a new, independent India.

Meanwhile, India had a new viceroy, Lord Willingdon, who was clamping down on all protests and boycotts. Not long after returning from his triumphant trip to Britain, Gandhi found himself in jail again.

The Untouchables

While Gandhi was in prison, he learned that if independence did go ahead, the British government was planning to hold separate elections for the Untouchables, the social outcasts at the bottom of Indian society.

Gandhi photographed during one of his many fasts. This picture shows how thin his lifestyle had made him.

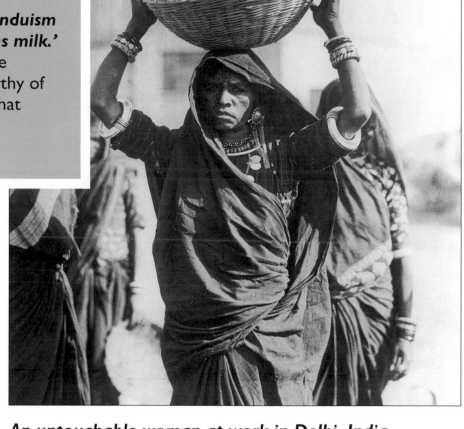

An untouchable woman at work in Delhi, India, in the early twentieth century.

He welcomed Untouchables (whom he called *harijans*, meaning 'Children of God') into his home, and even adopted a *harijan* girl, Lakshmi, as his daughter.

In September 1932, Gandhi decided to support the Untouchables by going on a hunger strike to force the British to change their plans. For a week he refused all food and drink, and grew close to death. His state of health was headline news all over India, and the taboos of the caste system were broken as high-caste and *harijan* people ate and waited together.

Finally, the British gave in, and Gandhi lived. However, the caste system itself was not destroyed so easily, and Untouchability still exists today.

A Break from Politics

When Gandhi came out of prison in 1933, he decided to leave politics for a while. He gave his ashram to the Untouchables and in 1934 he resigned as a member of the Indian National Congress. He left his friend Jawaharlal Nehru, the new Congress leader, to manage the political campaign, and became a wandering traveller again.

Gandhi speaking at a conference in Calcutta in 1934.

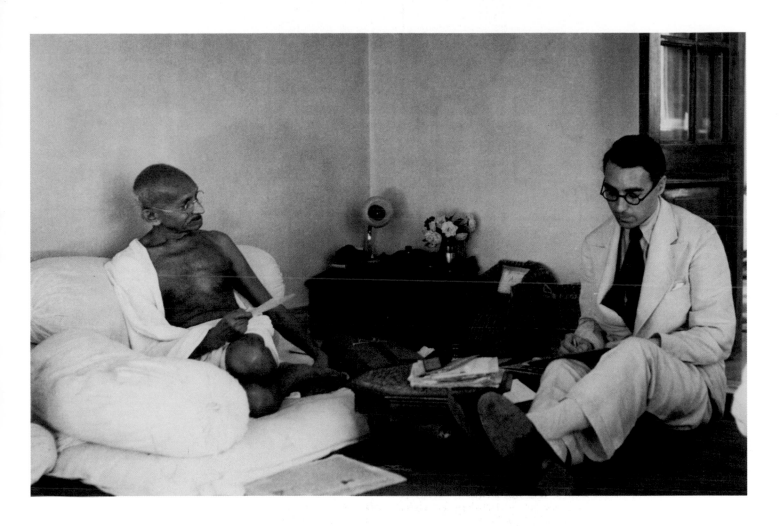

This time, however, he was world-famous, and followers and reporters came from around the globe to see him. He promised his friends that he would return to politics, when he felt the time was right.

In 1939, the Second World War broke out. Gandhi used his powerful voice to call for non-violence, but to no effect.

As a British territory, India was an important barrier between Germany and its Japanese allies. The Indian National Congress promised to support the war effort, in return for independence as soon as the war ended. Many world leaders urged Britain to agree, but the new British leader, Winston Churchill, hated the thought of losing India from the British empire.

Gandhi being interviewed by Robert Stimson, a journalist for Picture Post, *in 1940. By this time Gandhi's name was known throughout the world.*

'Never give in. Never. Never. Never. Never.' This quotation from the mid-20th-century British prime minister, Winston Churchill, displays his stubborn attitude to problems.

33

'Quit India!'

In April 1942, in the middle of the war, Gandhi decided to start campaigning again. His new slogan was 'Quit India!', and he called for an immediate, non-violent revolution. But he and the leaders of the Indian National Congress soon found themselves in prison yet again, while rioting, terrorism and police violence became worse across India.

Gandhi at the flower-strewn deathbed of his wife Kasturbai in 1944.

This was an enormous disappointment for Gandhi, as he longed for a peaceful, non-violent outcome. His misery was made even worse in 1944 when Kasturbai, who had stood by him for 62 years, caught acute bronchitis. He was allowed to leave jail briefly to visit her deathbed, and she died in his arms. Gandhi then became ill himself. Churchill, sure he was about to die, had him released from jail.

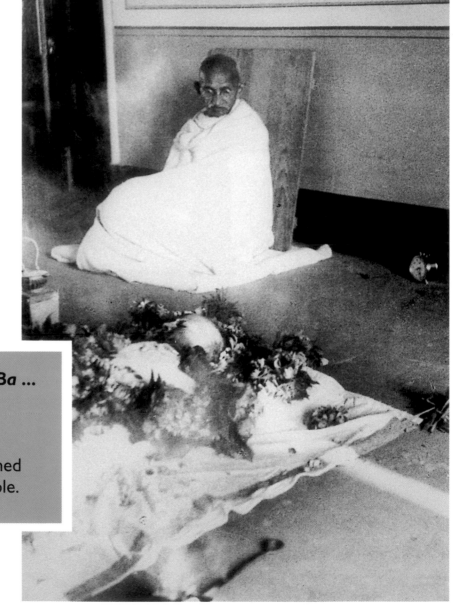

'I cannot imagine life without Ba ... her passing has left a vacuum which will never be filled.'
Gandhi on the death of his wife Kasturbai, who had been nicknamed 'Ba' ('Mother') by the Indian people.

But there was light at the end of the tunnel. Gandhi survived, the war ended, and a new Labour government came to power in Britain. One of its priorities was to arrange independence for India.

Left **Gandhi on his way to an Indian National Congress committee meeting. Despite his grief at Kasturbai's death, he continued to work towards independence for India.**

Right **Gandhi with Jawaharlal Nehru, his close friend and political ally, who became leader of the Indian National Congress.**

Independence at Last

Britain was ready to leave India and let Indians rule themselves. The only trouble was, no one could agree on exactly how the country should be run. A conference was held in Simla in 1945 to discuss the problem, but it didn't help. Britain wanted to give power to the mainly Hindu Indian National Congress, led by Jawaharlal Nehru. But Ali Jinnah, leader of a Muslim organization called the Muslim League, wanted India's Muslims to have their own, 'pure' Muslim state.

After the conference, Hindus and Muslims all over India began fighting and killing each other. Gandhi, who did not believe any one religion was better than any other, went on the road again, making speeches and calling for the violence to stop.

Ali Jinnah, the Muslim leader who demanded a new, separate country for India's Muslims. That country was Pakistan, which was founded when India became independent.

'God is not in Kaaba or in Kashi. He is within
every one of us.'
Gandhi opposing religious riots in India. He believed
that all religions were really the same and shared the
same God. (Kaaba is a Muslim holy site and Kashi is
a Hindu holy site. Both are in India.)

*Violence between
Hindus and Muslims
swept India in the late
1940s. This photo shows
riots in Bombay in 1946.*

Finally, in 1947, the British government made a decision.
Britain would leave India by June 1948. There was still no
solution, but it would have to be sorted out in time.

Partition

Ali Jinnah, the leader of the Muslim League, was determined to establish a separate country for the Muslims. He threatened to start a civil war if his demands weren't met. India was about to be divided.

Sooner than expected, on 15 August 1947, the Indian National Congress acted. They raised the new Indian flag (a modified version of the Indian National Congress flag) in Delhi, India's capital. Nehru made an independence speech;

This map shows the movement of Muslims and Hindus during Partition. Other places mentioned in this book are also shown.

'We Indians are one as no two Englishmen are.' Gandhi opposing Partition. He saw India as a united whole, and couldn't bear the idea of Indians turning against one another.

but Gandhi was nowhere to be seen. He had gone to Calcutta, still on his mission to stop Hindu-Muslim riots.

Thousands of Muslims began streaming towards the mainly-Muslim north-west corner of India, which (along with what is now Bangladesh) was to become Pakistan. Meanwhile, Hindus trapped in the new 'pure' Muslim state fled back to India. This process, which took place in the later months of 1947, was known as Partition. Over a million people lost their lives in the fighting between Muslims and Hindus. Gandhi, the non-violent revolutionary, was devastated.

Muslims cling to a refugee train heading for Pakistan shortly after Partition. Trains taking Muslims and Hindus to their new homes were often attacked by the opposing side.

A Violent Death

Gandhi had managed to calm the riots in Calcutta, and returned to Delhi, where he stayed with a friend. He continued to call for peace between religions, and even fasted again to try to stop the fighting. But many Hindus and Muslims turned against him, each accusing him of supporting the other side. On 20 January 1948, a bomb was thrown at the house where he was staying. Gandhi was unhurt, but the message was clear.

Gandhi with his great-nieces Abha and Manu. After his wife's death, they were his assistants and constant companions.

Just ten days later, on 30 January, Gandhi walked out of his house to go to a prayer meeting, along with his two great-nieces, Abha and Manu. In the crowd waiting for him was Nathuram Godse, a Hindu newspaper editor and strong supporter of the Hindus.

Suddenly Godse darted out of the crowd and pushed past Manu. He took out a pistol and shot Gandhi three times. According to witnesses, Gandhi sank to the ground, breathing the words '*He Rama*'— meaning 'Oh God'— before he died.

Nathuram Godse (in the front row, on the right) in the dock, accused of the killing of Gandhi. With him are eight other men accused of taking part in a plan to murder the Mahatma.

'**Death is at any time blessed, but it is twice blessed for a warrior who dies for his cause, that is, truth.**' Gandhi on death. He was seventy-eight at the time of his death.

Farewell to 'Bapu'

Gandhi's friend Jawaharlal Nehru was now independent India's first prime minister. As soon as he heard of Gandhi's death, he rushed to Delhi, and that evening he announced the news on India's national radio station. The whole country was plunged into mourning.

Gandhi's ashes are carried to the River Ganges on a decorated chariot, surrounded by mourners.

'The light has gone out of our lives, and there is darkness everywhere... Our beloved leader, Bapu, as we call him, the Father of our Nation, is no more.'
Jawaharlal Nehru broadcasting the news of Gandhi's assassination on 30 January, 1948.

Indian cabinet ministers set sail to scatter Gandhi's ashes on the holy waters of the Ganges and Jumna rivers.

Godse, Gandhi's assassin, had not tried to escape. He was quickly arrested and pleaded guilty to the killing, for which he was eventually executed.

Gandhi was given a traditional Hindu funeral. His body was washed, covered with flowers and carried through the streets to a sandalwood funeral pyre, where a crowd of over two million people watched it burn. Ten days later, the ashes were scattered at the meeting point of India's two holiest rivers, the Ganges and the Jumna.

Gandhi's Legacy

Today, Gandhi is remembered around the world. His distinctive appearance has made him one of the most easily recognized leaders of all time. But what exactly did he leave behind?

Although he is sometimes treated like a saint, Gandhi did not see himself as a religious leader. And although he led India to independence, he was not a politician. He didn't even achieve his aims — India's independence came at a terrible cost in violence and suffering.

Nelson Mandela, who campaigned for racial freedom in South Africa, was awarded the Gandhi Peace Prize in the year 2000. Many people thought Gandhi should have won the Nobel Peace Prize, although he never did. After his death, the Indian government set up the Gandhi Peace Prize in his honour.

Yet Gandhi showed the world how effective non-violent protest could be. His philosophy of love, peace and forgiveness, between people of different religions, races and beliefs has inspired many struggles for freedom around the world. And his words of wisdom, preserved in his writings and recalled by his friends, continue to inspire us today.

This statue of Gandhi on his salt march stands in the centre of New Delhi, India.

'Where there is love, there is life; hatred leads to destruction.' One of Gandhi's most famous quotations, summing up his belief in non-violence, forgiveness and the power of love.

45

Glossary

Aristocrat A member of the elite or ruling classes.

Ashram A communal dwelling founded by a spiritual leader.

Boycott To refuse to buy goods or services as a way of making a protest.

Campaign A series of protests and activities designed to bring about change.

Caste system A traditional Indian social system which divides society into many different levels, or *jati*.

Charkha An Indian spinning wheel.

Civil disobedience Refusal to obey the laws or commands of the government.

Civil war A war between two groups inside the same country.

Curfew A ban on going outdoors, usually imposed at night.

Fast To go without food for a certain period of time.

Harijan Gandhi's name for Untouchables. The word means 'Children of God'.

Hindu A member of the Hindu religion. Hindus believe in many different gods.

Jati see caste system.

Khadi An Indian word for plain, homespun cloth.

Lynch To kill someone as a punishment, without the approval of the law.

Mahatma A Sanskrit (ancient Indian) word which means 'Great Soul'.

Muslim A member of Islam, a religion that has one God.

Petition A written request to the government, often signed by many people.

Philosopher A person who thinks deeply about what life means.

Pyre A bonfire for burning a dead body.

Satyagraha A word invented by Gandhi to describe non-violent, peaceful resistance. It translates as 'truth-force'.

Strike To refuse to work as a form of protest.

Swaraj An Indian word for independence.

Terrorism Violent and illegal acts performed to protest against laws or attitudes.

Untouchables The lowest members of society, according to the caste system.

Vaishya The *jati* or caste 'level' that Gandhi was born into.

Viceroy Someone who rules in place of a monarch. A British viceroy governed India when it was in the British Empire.

Further Information

Books to read

Younger readers:
Gandhi by Pratima Mitchell (Oxford University Press, 1997)

Older readers:
Livewire Real Lives: Mahatma Gandhi by Mike Wilson (Hodder & Stoughton, 1996)

Sources
Gandhi: Father of a Nation by Catherine Clément (Thames & Hudson, 1989)
Gandhi by Yogesh Chadha (John Wiley & Sons, 1997)

Date Chart

1869, 2 October Mohandas Karamchand Gandhi born in Porbandar, Porbandar State, India.

1882 Married Kasturbai Makanji in an arranged Hindu wedding.

1885 Gandhi's father dies. His own first child is born, but dies a few days later.

1888 Gandhi's son Harilal is born.

1888 Goes to London to study law.

1891 Returns to India as a qualified lawyer.

1892 Gandhi's son Manilal is born.

1893, April Sails to South Africa to work as a lawyer and encounters racial prejudice during a train journey.

1894 Founds the Natal Indian Congress to fight for the rights of Indians in South Africa.

1897 Gandhi's son Ramdas is born.

1900 Gandhi's son Devadas is born.

1903 Builds first ashram near Durban, South Africa.

1906 Develops concept of *Satyagraha*, or truth-force.

1913, September Leads final South African campaign, resulting in improved conditions for Indian workers.

1915 Returns to India with family. Founds a new ashram near Ahmedabad and becomes a wandering traveller.

1918 Fasts in order to win rights for Ahmedabad textile workers.

1920 Begins nationwide campaign urging people to boycott British goods and weave their own cloth.

1922-24 Spends two years in jail.

1925 Elected president of Indian National Congress.

1929 Indian National Congress declares India independent without British consent.

1930 Leads 'salt march' to gather salt illegally from the beach at Dandi.

1932 Fasts in order to win rights for Untouchables.

1934 Resigns from Indian National Congress and travels around India.

1942 Launches 'Quit India' campaign and urges Britian to grant India independence. Is immediately sent to jail.

1944 Gandhi's wife Kasturbai dies. He becomes ill and is released from jail.

1947 Britain agrees to grant India full independence and promises to leave the country by June 1948. Gandhi goes to Calcutta to campaign against violent riots.

1947, 15 August The Indian National Congress raises a new Indian flag in Delhi.

1947 Over a million die as the country is divided into India and Pakistan.

1948, 30 January Gandhi is shot dead in Delhi by Nathuram Godse.

Index

All numbers in **bold** refer to pictures as well as text.